photo-fabric
play

quilt & craft projects your whole family will love

Krista Camacho Halligan

C&T PUBLISHING

Text copyright © 2008 by Krista Camacho Halligan
Artwork copyright © 2008 by C&T Publishing, Inc.

Publisher: Amy Marson

Creative Director: Gailen Runge

Acquisitions Editor: Jan Grigsby

Editor: Stacy Chamness

Technical Editor: Susan Nelsen

Copyeditor/Proofreader: Wordfirm Inc.

Cover & Book Designer: Christina D. Jarumay

Page Layout Artist: Kerry Graham

Production Coordinators: Zinnia Heinzmann and
Kiera Lofgreen

Illustrator: Kirstie L. Pettersen

Photography by Luke Mulks, Diane Pedersen, and
Christina Carty-Francis of C&T Publishing unless
otherwise noted

Published by C&T Publishing, Inc., P.O. Box 1456,
Lafayette, CA 94549

Library of Congress Cataloging-in-Publication Data

Halligan, Krista Camacho,

Photo-fabric play : quilt & craft projects your whole
family will love / Krista Camacho Halligan.

    p. cm.

Summary: "Printing words and treasured family photos
onto fabric to use in projects puts a wonderful, personal
touch on the item. Book features wallhangings, a growth
chart, puzzle blocks, and more"--Provided by publisher.

ISBN 978-1-57120-559-9 (paper trade : alk. paper)

1. Quilts--Design. 2. Patchwork--Patterns. 3.
Photographs on cloth. I. Title. II. Title: Photo-fabric play,
quilt and craft projects your whole family will love.

TT835.H3328 2008

746.46'041--dc22

                          2007052476

Printed in China

10 9 8 7 6 5 4 3 2

acknowledgments

This book is dedicated with all my love to my favorite small people in the whole, wide world—Allison, Ava, and Liam. Always remember that joy truly does come from the little things.

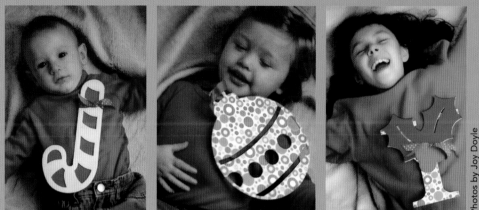

Photos by Joy Doyle

a huge thank you to:

Sue Astroth—for your untiring willingness to lend a hand, eye, or ear as a constant friend and artistic advisor, not to mention the spectacular scrapbook quilt.

Stacy Chamness—for your divine talents as an editorial genius . . . you goddess, you!

Lynn Koolish—for the marvelous *I Can Read* quilt and *My Favorite Things* wallhanging.

Phyllis Nelson—for your continued friendship, support, and encouragement. I'd only be a fraction of the artist I am today had I not met you. Also, for the beautiful *You're A Doll* project.

Debby DeBenedetti—for being someone who inspires and challenges me to new artistic levels, and for the magnificent scrapbook layout.

Vanessa Cole—for being a creative inspiration and wonderful friend. Also, for your fabulous work on the puzzle blocks.

Elaine Beattie—for your wonderful, speedy quilting and willingness to offer marvelous ideas.

Wendy, Joshie, and Lori Larks—for your constant support and friendship and a whole lot of play dates.

Julie Heald Adelson—for your friendship and play dates during the creation of this book.

Aimee Moss and Laurie Abbey—for all the Co-Op babysitting during the creation of this book.

Tasha Camacho—for all the memories and support throughout the years. ". . . just keep swim-ming, just keep swimming."

Dad, Kaoru, Josh, and Tino—for your love and for just being my family.

Mom—for being so proud of all I do.

Joey—for thinking that publishing this book makes me a celebrity.

Mitchell—for everything and always.

contents

introduction

collecting, combining & creating

I love collecting the treasures that accompany any given moment and telling a story with the photos and ephemera that go along with that memory. I love the idea that someday, someone who remembers me fondly might retell my stories when I am long gone. You can never have enough of these types of treasures, so making them for my own family is very important to me. This also gives me an excuse to be a packrat of sorts. I save the things that I hope will be cherished by my children in years to come: silly things like sticky notes with loving messages, report cards, artwork, movie or event ticket stubs . . . anything sentimental that I can get my hands on, really.

I was drawn to the art of scrapbooking many years ago by this idea of having personal treasures to pass down to members of my family. Collecting photos and combining them with personal mementos, stories, and other ephemera to create your family story with an artistic twist is wonderfully special. With the addition of digital images, scanners, and printers, I can finally combine my collections of ephemera, photos, artwork, and other sentimental items into beautiful pieces to pass on to my family for many generations to come. I can scan original pieces of my children's artwork to make a wallhanging. I can print photos on fabric to make a beautiful quilt or growth chart. I can make interactive wallhangings and other toys that my children can enjoy now, then pass on to their children. I can even scan toys that are special to them and make fabulous treasures, such as quilts or wallhangings, featuring their favorite things.

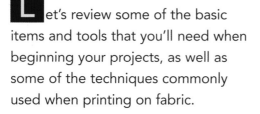

getting started

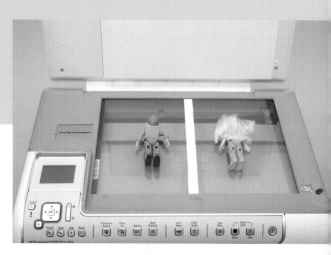

Let's review some of the basic items and tools that you'll need when beginning your projects, as well as some of the techniques commonly used when printing on fabric.

digital images, photos & other objects

Digital images, as well as photos and other scannable objects, are required for completing projects. You can print directly from your digital photo files, or you can scan or copy other photos. Flat objects, such as children's artwork, letters, notes, cards, and much more, can be scanned for use in your projects. Three-dimensional objects, such as favorite toys are also great to scan.

printer & scanner

Creating any of the projects featured in this book requires a printer and a scanner, at minimum. I use a printer that also includes a scanner and a copier, but many other types of scanners and inkjet printers are available. They are simple to operate and offer a wide variety of ways to scan, manipulate, and save your images to create perfectly personalized projects. A printer with the ability to print edge-to-edge without margins is especially desirable for projects.

WHAT CAN YOU SCAN?

Look around your home and you'll find many objects that can be scanned and included in your projects. Old photos, flowers, leaves, children's drawings, letters, cards, food items, favorite toys, and small pieces of clothing are among the many things that can be scanned to create beautifully personal pieces. It is important to be mindful of copyright laws. Some images are copyright protected, so if you plan on gifting or selling your items, it is best to scan images that are entirely your own.

software

Basic software programs, such as photo-editing software and word processing software, are needed for manipulating images and printing text. Photo-editing software will allow you to crop, resize, adjust color, and apply filters and effects to your images before printing. Word processing software will allow you to add text to your projects. Before beginning your projects, it's a good idea to familiarize yourself with your software programs. Different programs perform similar functions in different ways, so the programs I use may vary slightly from those that you have on your computer.

sewing machine

A sewing machine is required to complete many, but not all, of these projects. Take some time to familiarize yourself with your machine before starting your project. Be sure that your machine is properly cleaned and oiled, according to the manufacturer's instructions. Experiment with the stitch length and width to ensure that you know what your machine is capable of and what the outcome will be. You should be familiar enough with your machine that you are able to change a needle, wind a bobbin, and adjust the tension to accommodate different fabric types. Taking the time to become acquainted with your sewing machine will save you time and frustration once you begin your projects.

printable fabric sheets

PRETREATED FABRIC SHEETS

Pretreated printable fabric sheets come in a wide variety of fibers for your projects. You can find silk, rayon, cotton, canvas, and many others. These fabric sheets also come with different options designed for specific project applications. For example, you can find plain fabric sheets for sewing, fusible or iron-on fabric sheets for quick no-sew projects, and peel-and-stick sheets that are great for scrapbooks and other craft projects. Experiment with the different options to see what works best in your particular project.

PREPARE YOUR OWN FABRIC SHEETS

Preparing your own printable fabric sheets provides greater range of flexibility and creativity than using purchased pretreated sheets, and it also costs less. This method allows you to choose from any natural fabric, providing a range of color and texture options.

You can quickly and easily prepare your own fabric sheets for printing by using a product such as Bubble Jet Set 2000 (Sources, page 46). Treating your fabric ensures that your inkjet inks are permanent and colorfast when washed. No matter which product you choose, follow the manufacturer's instructions for best results.

Once the fabric has been treated, a backing is required to allow the fabric to pass through the printer. An iron-on stabilizer or freezer paper ironed onto the back of the fabric should be applied. Alternatively, $8\frac{1}{2}'' \times 11''$ shipping labels or full-size laser printer adhesive labels can be used. After the fabric is stabilized, cut it into pieces that will fit through your printer. For most printers, this will be a standard $8\frac{1}{2}'' \times 11''$ size.

paper

It is advisable to test your images on paper prior to printing on fabric. This will save you a lot of frustration, as you can familiarize yourself with the proper way to load the fabric sheet into your printer (fabric side up or fabric side down). Some printers carry your sheet up and over, inverting the page as it prints, while other printers draw paper straight in from the paper tray and then feed it straight out as it is being printed.

> ✱ *tip* *Determine which direction your printer feeds the paper by making a large mark across one side of your paper, loading the paper with the marked side face down, and printing. If you see the mark on the printed side, you'll know that you will have to load your fabric sheets with the fabric side down in order to get the desired results.*

scanning
photos &
flat objects

Many all-in-one printers can be used to either scan or photocopy your images and objects. What's the difference between scanning and photocopying?

If you choose to scan your image or object, the image is saved on your computer and can be manipulated, using software, prior to printing. Scanning allows you to apply a wide variety of effects to your image. You can modify colors, lighten or darken, sharpen, and crop or resize your image, to name just a few options.

If you choose to photocopy your image or object, your image is printed immediately and not saved for later manipulation. Photocopying allows you to print multiple copies of the same image on a single sheet, adjust image size, adjust tone and color intensity, or print black-and-white images rather than color. Try experimenting with your all-in-one printer to determine which option works best for your particular project.

who loves ava?
—wallhanging

Finished size: 22″ × 22″

I guess the real question should be who doesn't love the special little one in your life? This is for Ava to keep photos close at hand to remind her of the many special people who love her. While some of these people are close by and others are far away, it's always exciting to see your children recognize and remember the people that are important to them.

what you'll need

- 9 photos (each about 4″ × 4″)
- 3 pretreated printable fabric sheets, 8½″ × 11″
- Magnetic board in unfinished 22″ × 22″ wood frame with 4″ molding
- 9 magnetic tins 3½″ diameter with lids (Creative Imaginations)
- 2 sheets of cardstock 8½″ × 11″
- 24 feet 2″-wide foil tape (3M)
- Stylus
- Rubber brayer
- Die-cut machine with alphabet and heart dies
- Xyron machine with adhesive cartridge

- Selection of alcohol-based inks (Ranger Industries)
- Felt applicator (Ranger Industries)
- Alcohol Blending Solution (Ranger Industries)
- Cotton swabs
- Craft knife
- Metal ruler

how-to

1. Print 4 different photos per sheet onto pretreated printable fabric sheets following the manufacturer's instructions. Print a total of 9 photos.

2. Trim photos to fit inside the tins. Replace the covers. Set these aside for later.

3. To work on the frame, remove the magnet board from inside the frame.

4. Use cardstock with the die-cut machine to cut the appropriate lettering and hearts for your title and names.

5. Using the Xyron machine, apply adhesive to the die-cut letters and hearts, then apply them to the frame.

6. Measure 12 strips of foil tape each 24″ long for covering the frame. Each side of the frame uses 3 pieces of foil tape.

7. Center the first foil strip along the center of one side, over the die-cut letters, wrapping both ends around to the back.

8. Use the rubber brayer to press foil tape onto the frame, revealing the impression of the letters underneath.

9. Using a metal ruler and a craft knife, trim each end of the foil tape at 45° angles in relation to the frame corners.

10. Align a second foil strip with the edge of the first strip to cover around the outside edge of the frame on this side. Be careful not to overlap the edges of the foil strips. Use the brayer to press the foil to the frame and trim the strip to the proper angle at each end. Repeat to cover the inside edge of the frame's side.

11. Repeat Steps 7–10 to cover the remaining 3 sides of the frame.

12. Use a stylus to outline all letters and shapes.

tip *If you find that your stylus does not move smoothly over the foil tape, rub the section with waxed paper before outlining.*

13. Use the felt applicator to apply the alcohol inks to the foil tape until you achieve your desired effect.

14. Once the alcohol inks are dry, use the alcohol blending solution and cotton swabs to remove ink from the embossed letters and shapes.

tip *A few drops of alcohol blending solution go a very long way, so use it sparingly. If you accidentally get solution on other parts of the frame, you can always touch it up by applying more alcohol ink.*

15. Apply alcohol inks to the magnetic board to tint, if desired.

16. To complete the project, secure the magnetic board inside the frame and add the metal tins.

alli—i'll love you forever
—scrapbook quilt

By Sue Astroth
Finished size: 18½″ × 21½″

This is the perfect way to display your little one's photos along with fabric, embellishments, a personal message, and any other mementos you'd like to add. You can select fabric to match the child's room decor, creating a decorative wallhanging of your special memory. While Alli is quite a bit older now than she was in these photos, she'll be able to cherish this memory of the park near her Grandma's house, and she can even pass it along to her own children one day.

what you'll need

- 4 photos
- 1 pretreated printable fabric sheet, 8½″ × 11″
- Variety of fabric scraps for the quilt top
- 20″ × 24″ piece of fabric for backing
- 20″ × 24″ piece of batting
- 2 yards ¼″-wide double-faced satin ribbon in colors to match fabrics (Offray)
- Several cardstock sheets, 12″ × 12″ to match fabrics
- Chipboard alphabet
- Chipboard flower (Bazzill Basics)
- Metal embellishments (Marcella and Making Memories)
- Mini spiral paper clip (Creative Impressions)
- Paper flowers (Making Memories)
- Heart charm
- Vintage ladybug pin (or something similar, if desired)
- Tacky glue

cutting instructions

Press all fabric before cutting pieces.

For the quilt center, cut:

1 rectangle 10½″ × 13½″ (**A**)

For the inner border, cut:

2 strips 2″ × 13½″ (**B**)

2 strips 2″ × 10½″ (**C**)

4 squares 2″ × 2″ (**D**)

For the outer border, cut:

2 strips 3″ × 16½″ (**E**)

2 strips 3″ × 13½″ (**F**)

4 squares 3″ × 3″ (**G**)

For the backing, cut:

1 rectangle 20″ × 24″

how-to

SEWING THE QUILT

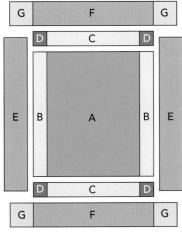

Quilt Layout

1. Using a ¼″ seam allowance throughout, sew a strip **B** to each side of center piece **A**. Finger-press seam allowance toward the center piece.

2. For the pieced top and bottom inner border, sew a **D** to each end of both **C** pieces and press the seams toward the outside.

3. Attach the pieced borders to the top and bottom of piece **A**.

4. Sew an **E** strip to each side of the quilt top. Press the seams toward the center.

5. For the pieced top and bottom outer border, sew a **G** to each end of both **F** pieces and press the seams toward the outside.

6. Attach the pieced borders to the top and bottom of the quilt and press the seams to the outside.

7. Place the batting on the table in front of you. Lay the backing piece face up on the top of the batting. Lightly press.

8. Lay the pieced top face down on the backing fabric. Pin.

9. Sew around the edge of the quilt top using a ¼″ seam allowance, but leaving a 2½″ to 3″ opening at the bottom of the quilt for turning right side out. Trim away excess fabric, batting, and threads—very close to the seam allowance to minimize bulk.

10. Clip corners diagonally. Turn the quilt right side out and lightly press. Pin the opening closed and sew by hand with a hidden stitch.

11. To hold the layers together, machine quilt around the quilt ¼″ from edge. Also, quilt in-the-ditch, right along the seam allowances, between the 2 borders and center fabric. (For more quilting tips, see Quilting Basics, page 44.)

EMBELLISHING THE QUILT

Read through all the instructions first before you start sewing your embellishments to your quilt. These instructions show you how to make this project exactly as it is pictured, but you may want to experiment with your own layout, placing your collected embellishments and photos on your quilt in a design pleasing to your eye. If you decide to use your own arrangement, it's a good idea to roughly sketch the layout plan on a piece of paper. This way, you will remember where everything should go once you have removed it all from the quilt.

1. Here's the layout that I used. You can refer to the project photo for greater detail. Refer to the photo sizes below so you can plan the photos on your fabric sheet. Print the 4 photos on the pretreated printable fabric, following the manufacturer's instructions. Trim the photos to the following sizes:

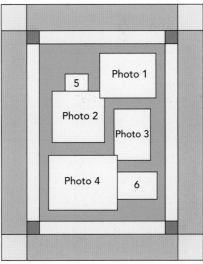

Photo 1—4¼″ × 3¼″

Photo 2—4″ × 3¾″

Photo 3—2¾″ × 3¾″

Photo 4—5¼″ × 4″

2. None of the photos are sewn directly to the quilt. First sew the photos to a contrasting cardstock mat about ½″ larger than the photo dimensions. Sew through the cardstock just like it's fabric. Be sure to have a sharp needle and set your machine to 10 stitches per inch. You can see that I double matted Photo 4.

> ✳ *tip* *Your sewing lines are also part of your quilt's various embellishments. You can use a contrasting color thread or a zigzag stitch to highlight the border your stitches will create. If you are afraid your sewn line won't be straight, go around the piece twice, making subtle bumps and curves as you go. Practice on a scrap to get the hang of it . . . I just love the finished look of this style.*

3. Referring to the diagram (page 11), sew a piece of cardstock, slightly smaller than each photo, directly onto the quilt. Do this for all 4 photos.

4. To my eye, the cardstock (pieces 5 and 6) help fill the center of the quilt. Sew cardstock pieces in these spots slightly smaller than the actual pieces that you plan to use, just as you did for the photos in Step 3. Follow my tip for preparing embellishments for the quilt.

> ✳ *tip* *To hide your stitches, sew a scrap piece of cardstock—slightly smaller than the piece you need to attach to the quilt—right where you want to add your embellishment. Glue your embellishment to a little bit larger piece of cardstock with a thin layer of good-quality tacky glue. Let it dry and you are good to go! This will be added to the wallhanging in Step 6.*

5. To make the name, use chipboard, metal letters, some die cuts, and a few randomly cut squares of cardstock. Sew each piece of cardstock directly onto the quilt top, with the exception of the flower.

> ✳ *tip* *The chipboard flower was too thick to go through a sewing machine so I drilled holes in the center of the flower and attached it just like a large button.*

6. Glue the matted photos and matted embellishments to the sewn cardstock on the quilt, using tacky glue. Because of the slight overlap of photos, attach Photos 2 and 3 first. (If you used your own layout instead, note that the number and sizes of the photos you use may change the order you need to follow.)

7. Add additional embellishments, ribbons, and letters directly to the top of the flower and other squares of cardstock.

8. Be sure to sign and date your masterpiece! (I usually sign on the back of the quilt.)

> ✳ *note* *If you have a story to tell about the photos used on your quilt, include it in an envelope attached to the back of your quilt. That way details such as places, dates, and names won't be forgotten.*

For more scrapbook quilts, see Fast, Fun & Easy Scrapbook Quilts *by Sue Astroth (C&T Publishing).*

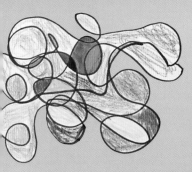

art-of-the-week

—wallhanging

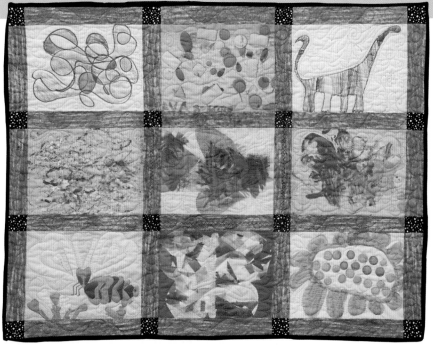

Original artwork by Allison and Ava Halligan
Finished size: 38″ × 30½″

As the parent of a preschooler, I find that art projects are abundant. It seems that there is a never-ending supply of paper covered in paint, markers, crayon, foam pieces, feathers, popsicle sticks, glitter, and whatever else your creative little ones can get their hands on. I am a true lover of this art and feel huge amounts of guilt when discarding any of these treasures. The problem is that many of these works of art are done on highly acidic paper, making preservation difficult for the art-loving mom. This project is a wonderful solution to this problem. Scan and preserve your favorite art pieces, make a beautiful wallhanging, and you'll always have a place to display the art of the week.

what you'll need

This project requires a printer that has the ability to print edge-to-edge on 8½″ × 11″ paper. If your printer can only print within margins, this wallhanging can still be done, but you will have to adjust the cut dimensions to fit your printed art blocks.

- 9 pieces of your favorite artwork for scanning
- 16 pretreated printable fabric sheets, 8½″ × 11″
- ⅛ yard of black dot fabric for sashing stones

- ⅓ yard for binding
- 1 yard for quilt backing
- 42″ × 34″ piece of batting
- 1 sheet Quilter's Vinyl, 10″ × 13″ (C&T Publishing)
- 1 sheet white paper, 8½″ × 11″
- Black crayon

how-to

1. Scan 9 pieces of children's artwork. Resize and adjust as necessary to fill the sheet for printing.

2. Print the artwork on pretreated fabric sheets, according to the manufacturer's instructions. Each of these 9 sheets is a piece **A**.

3. Color in a single direction with your black crayon until you cover the entire sheet of plain white paper.

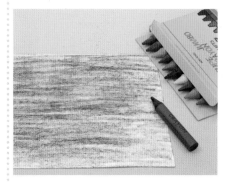

4. Scan the crayon-colored paper and print 6 copies onto pretreated fabric sheets.

5. Cut each of the 6 printed fabric sheets into 4 strips 2″ × 11″, making 24 strips total. From these strips, 12 strips are called piece **B**.

6. Trim the remaining 12 strips to 2″ × 8½″. This is piece **C**.

7. Cut 16 squares 2″ × 2″ from the black dot fabric. This is piece **D**.

8. Lay out all the **A**, **B**, **C**, and **D** pieces, following the quilt layout. Make a pleasing arrangement of all the artworks.

D	B	D	B	D	B	D
C	A	C	A	C	A	C

Quilt Layout

9. Using a ¼″ seam, sew each row together and then join the rows to complete the quilt top.

10. Layer the backing, batting, and finished quilt top.

11. Quilt as desired and bind with the black fabric. (For quilting and binding tips, see Quilting Basics, page 44.)

12. Place the 10″ × 13″ sheet of Quilter's Vinyl over the center block and sew the left, right, and bottom edges of the Quilter's Vinyl over the center block, using a large zigzag stitch as shown.

13. Slip your little one's latest artwork into the pocket for display!

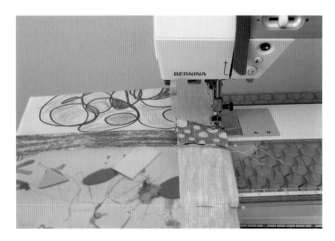

> **✳ tip** *A couple pins placed along the seam you are about to sew helps keep all your fabrics and seams aligned. Be careful not to sew over them, as it can break the pin and/or needle.*

create yourself
—scrapbook layout

By Debby DeBenedetti
Finished size: 24″ × 12″

This lovely scrapbook layout celebrates an Easter egg hunt. By combining images printed on paper with those printed on canvas and cotton poplin, the layout illustrates the creative contrast of various fabrics and traditional paper photography. Stitched frames accentuate the fabric images.

what you'll need

- 4 photos
- 1 pretreated cotton poplin fabric peel-and-stick sheet, 8½″ × 11″
- 1 pretreated canvas fabric peel-and-stick sheet, 8½″ × 11″
- 1 heavyweight matte photo paper sheet, 8½″ × 11″
- 6 complementary patterned papers, 12″ × 12″
- 3 complementary solid papers, 12″ × 12″
- 6 buttons
- 4″ of ¼″ ribbon (or more, if desired)
- 4″ of ½″ ribbon (or more, if desired)
- Alphabet stickers
- Green journaling block sticker, 2⅛″ × 3″
- Cream journaling block sticker, 1¾″ × 1¾″
- Striped frame sticker, 3″ × 3″ (SEI)
- Rub-on words for "create yourself" and "wish"
- Corner-rounder punch (EK Success)
- Stapler
- Sewing machine
- Adhesive (Herma Dotto for paper, Glue Dots for buttons)

how-to

PHOTO PREPARATION

1. Print the following photos according to the manufacturer's instructions:

   Photo 1—6¾" × 8½" printed on the poplin sheet

   Photo 2—5" × 5" printed on the heavyweight matte photo paper

   Photo 3—4¼" × 6½" printed on the heavyweight matte photo paper

   Photo 4—4¼" × 5" printed on the canvas sheet

2. Trim the photos to the sizes given in the instructions for each page.

LEFT PAGE CONSTRUCTION

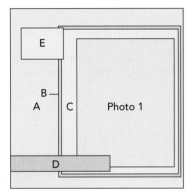

Left Page Layout
Photo 1—6¾" × 8½" (Ours is printed on a poplin sheet.)
A—12" × 12" decorative background paper
B—8½" × 10" patterned paper outer photo mat
C—8" × 9½" pink paper inner photo mat
D—7" × 1" accent patterned paper
E—Green journaling sticker

1. Trim all the papers (**A–D**) to the given sizes.

2. Mat Photo 1, using **B** as the outer border mat and **C** as the inner border. Notice that the photo is not centered on the mats.

3. Sew 2 sides of the frame around Photo 1 with a decorative stitch, sewing through the printable fabric and both photo mats.

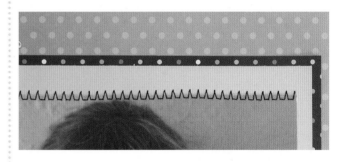

4. Refer to the left page diagram for placement and adhere the matted photo to background paper **A**.

5. Staple each ribbon length into a V-shape, side by side on the accent paper **D**.

6. Glue the accent paper at the bottom left-hand corner of the photo.

7. Glue buttons below the ribbons, using Glue Dots.

8. Journal on the green journaling block **E** and attach at the top left-hand side of the background paper.

9. Apply rub-on words "create yourself" as desired, according to the manufacturer's instructions.

> ✳ *tip* *Place rub-on over the desired area and rub using small, even strokes. As you are working, you can gently lift the corner of the completed portion to determine if all parts of rub-on have adhered to your fabric. If not, simply place the corner back down and rub places that have been missed. Never remove an entire rub-on sheet until you are sure the rub-on has transferred completely, as properly realigning the sheet is extremely difficult.*

RIGHT PAGE CONSTRUCTION

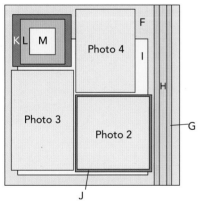

Right Page Layout

Photo 2—5″ × 5″ (Ours is printed on heavyweight matte photo paper.)

Photo 3—4¼″ × 6½″ (Ours is printed on heavyweight matte photo paper.)

Photo 4—4¼″ × 5″ (Ours is printed on a canvas sheet.)

F—12″ × 12″ decorative background paper

G—1⅛″ × 12″ border paper

H—½″ × 12″ border paper

I—9″ × 9″ cream paper montage background

J—5¼″ × 5¼″ photo border paper

K—4″ × 3½″ decorative paper mat

L—Striped frame sticker

M—Cream journal sticker

1. Trim all the papers (**F–K**) to the given sizes.

2. Glue the border paper strip **G** about ½″ from the right-hand edge of background paper **F**.

3. Center the narrow decorative paper strip **H** centered on top of decorative strip **G** and glue in place.

4. Round the top the corners of the photo montage paper **I**, using the corner-rounder punch. Place the montage paper ¼″ from the decorative strip and ½″ from the bottom of the page. Glue in place.

5. Mat Photo 2, using the photo border paper **J**.

6. Arrange Photos 2, 3, and 4 on top of photo montage paper **I**, leaving ⅛″ between photos. Glue in place.

7. Sew a frame around Photo 4 with a decorative stitch, sewing through the printable fabric and all the paper layers.

8. Apply the "wish" rub-on to Photo 4, according to the manufacturer's instructions.

9. Using the corner-rounder punch, round all corners of journaling mat paper **K** and place at top left-hand corner of page.

10. Add journaling to cream journal sticker **M**. Place this journal sticker on the striped frame **L** and attach it to the center of mat **K**.

11. To complete your page, place alphabet stickers on the frame and journal block in the upper left corner of the page.

12. These pages are now ready for your scrapbook!

let's learn the alphabet
—wallhanging

Finished size: 28˝ × 28˝

While playing with some flash cards with my children, I thought this project would be a great, decorative way to help little ones learn the alphabet. With these durable, fabric-fused cards, there is no longer any problem with your flash cards getting torn or crumpled, making it a perfect project for those with toddlers. Hook-and-loop tape backing on the cards makes learning the order of the alphabet fun and convenient. Realistic pictures on the cards make object recognition fun. For older children, scanning cards that have only one letter per card can turn this project into a great learn-to-spell tool. The possibilities are endless with this timeless decorative learning project.

what you'll need

- Alphabet flash cards to scan
- 4 pretreated printable fusible fabric sheets, 8½″ × 11″
- 1⅛ yards of alphabet fabric
- 1 yard of dotted fabric (includes binding)
- ⅞ yards for backing
- 1½ yards 28″-wide heavyweight fast2fuse
- ¾ yard 28″-wide regular-weight fast2fuse
- 26 hook-and-loop ½″ dots
- Nonstick appliqué pressing sheet

cutting instructions

Prior to assembling your wallhanging project, you'll need to gather the fabric and cut the pieces as follows:

From the heavyweight fast2fuse, cut:

    1 square 28″ × 28″

    4 rectangles 8½″ × 11″

From the alphabet fabric, cut:

    1 square 28″ × 28″

From the backing fabric, cut:

    1 square 28″ × 28″

From the dotted fabric, cut:

    4 strips 5″ × 25″

From the regular-weight fast2fuse, cut:

    4 strips 5″ × 25″

how-to

1. Scan flash cards 4 at a time.

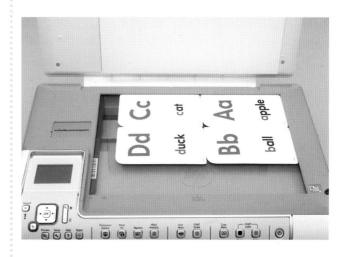

2. Print 2 scanned images (8 flash cards) on each 8½″ × 11″ fabric sheet.

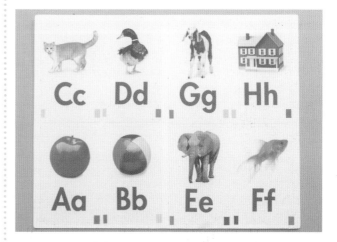

3. Using the pressing sheet, fuse the printed sheets to 8½″ × 11″ pieces of heavyweight fast2fuse, according to the manufacturer's instructions.

4. Trim each flash card to fit your project. (Mine measure 2½″ × 4″, but you can adjust yours accordingly.)

5. For the flash card backings, cut pieces of the alphabet fabric to fit the dimensions you chose. If you are using a directional print, be sure to pay attention to the orientation of the print. Sew the soft side of a hook-and-loop dot to the center of each backing piece.

6. Using the pressing sheet, fuse these pieces of alphabet fabric to the backs of the flash cards, according to the manufacturer's instructions. Sew a red zigzag around the card edges to finish. (I used a stitch length of 5 and width of 0.5. Experiment with your machine to get the look you like.)

7. Fuse the 28″ of heavyweight fast2fuse between the 28″ squares of alphabet fabric and the backing, according to the manufacturer's instructions. Again, use the pressing sheet.

8. Find the center line along the length of each dotted strip. Refer to the project photo (page 18) to ensure that 2 rows will have 7 flash cards and 2 rows will have 6 flash cards each. Sew the bristly side of the hook-and-loop dots along the center line of each dotted strip, spacing them accordingly.

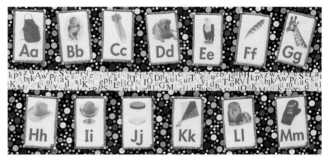

Make 2 rows of 6 cards and 2 rows of 7.

9. Fuse the 4 dotted strips to the 4 pieces 5″ × 25″ regular-weight fast2fuse, according to manufacturer's instructions. Fuse these strips to the front of the wall-hanging as shown in the project photo.

10. Use the remaining dotted fabric to bind the wallhanging. (For binding tips, see Quilting Basics, page 44.)

> ✳ *tip* For beginning readers, you can place a word on the front of the flash card with the corresponding image on the back.

scanning
3D objects

S canning three-dimensional objects is a great way to add personal treasured items to your artwork. Look around your home and you can find a wide variety of items that can be scanned. You can include favorite toys, jewelry, flowers, leaves, fruits, or anything else you can dream up. In the following projects, we scanned a variety of toys to make a reading quilt, and much-loved dress-up articles to make a favorite things wallhanging. There are so many ways that your scanned 3D items can be incorporated into your projects. Have fun!

i can read!

—quilt

By Lynn Koolish
Finished size: 38½″ × 38½″

Make learning fun with pictures and words. Scan objects that you have around the house—or use existing photos—and print the images on pretreated fabric sheets. When looking for items to scan**, it's best if they are all approximately the same size. Use a word processing program to write the corresponding words and print them on fabric that you treat with Bubble Jet Set 2000 yourself.

**When scanning, please respect copyright laws.

what you'll need

- 18 objects for scanning and printing
- 9 pretreated fabric sheets, 8½″ × 11″
- ½ yard of magenta for printed words

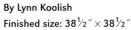

- ½ yard of light turquoise for printed words
- ½ yard of magenta print for border
- ⅓ yard of yellow print for sashing
- ¼ yard of dark turquoise for narrow inner border
- ⅓ yard for binding
- 1¼ yards for backing
- 43″ × 43″ batting
- 2½ yards 17″-wide fusible stabilizer or freezer paper
- Bubble Jet Set 2000

prepping and cutting instructions

1. Refer to "Prepare Your Own Fabric Sheets" on page 6 to treat and stabilize the magenta and light turquoise fabrics before cutting. Follow the manufacturer's instructions for the Bubble Jet Set 2000 and then stabilize both fabrics with the stabilizer of your choice before cutting.

2. Press all fabric before cutting pieces.

From the magenta, cut:

5 rectangles 8½″ × 11″

From the light turquoise, cut:

4 rectangles 8½″ × 11″

From the yellow print, cut:

6 strips 2″ × 9½″ for short sashing strips

2 strips 2″ × 30½″ for long sashing strips

From the dark turquoise, cut:

4 strips 1″ × width of fabric for narrow inner border

From the magenta print, cut:

4 strips 4″ × width of fabric for outer borders

how-to

1. To get the green tint on the pretreated fabric sheets, select a colored background paper or fabric and cut the paper to the dimensions of the white, inside portion of the scanner lid. Use removable, two-sided tape to temporarily secure this to the lid of the scanner to provide a colored background for the scanned object. Print items or photos on the pretreated fabric sheets, grouping 2 objects on a page so they can be trimmed to 5″ × 5″ squares.

> ✳ *tip* *If you have a transparency or acetate sheet, draw a line halfway across the sheet. Place the sheet on the scanner glass, so you can center your items on each half.*

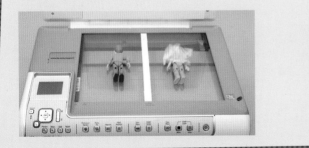

2. Use a word processing program to create the words and print them on the prepared colored fabrics sheets. Arrange the words so that 2 word squares, 5″ × 5″, can be cut from each sheet, with the word centered in each square.

3. Trim the printed objects and words to 5″ × 5″ squares.

4. Arrange the squares into 9 four-patch blocks, matching up the words with the objects. Arrange 5 magenta blocks and 4 turquoise blocks. Sew each four-patch together. Press all seams toward the green.

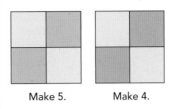

Make 5.   Make 4.

5. Refer to the quilt layout to arrange the blocks and sashing strips. Sew the short sashing strips between the blocks. Press the seam allowances toward the sashing.

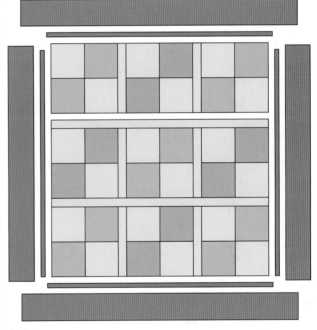

Quilt Layout

6. Sew the long sashing strips between the rows. Press the seam allowances toward the sashing.

7. Refer to Straight Cut Borders on page 44 to add the narrow dark turquoise borders strips and the magenta print outer border strips. Press all the seams toward the quilt center.

8. Layer the backing, batting, and quilt top.

9. Quilt as desired and bind the quilt. (For quilting and binding tips see Quilting Basics, page 44.)

my favorite things
—wallhanging
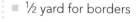

By Lynn Koolish
Finished size: 22″ × 22″
Photos by Krista Camacho Halligan

This easy to make quilt features photos of my favorite little ballerina and her props. The photos and frames are fused in place, making it easy for you to choose the number, size of photos, and placement that you want to use. The ribbons add a playful touch for this quilt, but you can choose embellishments that fit your little one's favorite things.

what you'll need

- 5 photos or items to scan
- 3–4 pretreated printable fusible fabric sheets, 8½″ × 11″
- 1 yard of purple for image frames and binding
- ¾ yard of pink for quilt center
- ½ yard for borders
- 1 yard for backing
- 34″ × 35″ piece of batting
- 1 yard of 17″-wide paper-backed fusible web
- Assorted ribbons and embellishments
- Nonstick appliqué pressing sheet

cutting the fabric

From the pink fabric, cut:

    1 rectangle 24½″ × 25½″

From the purple fabric (previously prepared with fusible web), cut:

    1 square 9½″ × 9½″

    1 rectangle 5½″ × 9½″

    2 rectangles 4″ × 6″

    2 rectangles 4″ × 3″

From the border fabric, cut:

    2 strips 3½″ × 24½″ for top and bottom borders

    2 strips 3½″ × 32″ for side borders

how-to

1. Copy or print photos onto pretreated, fusible fabric sheets, according to the manufacturer's instructions. Scan images for project. Group the images to be printed whenever possible to ensure the most efficient use of fabric sheets. You'll need the following sizes:

> Image for upper center—4″ × 8″
>
> Image for upper sides (printed twice)—4″ × 3″
>
> Image for left side—4″ × 6″
>
> Image for right side—4″ × 6″
>
> Image for lower center—8″ × 8″

2. Trim images to the given sizes on page 22.

SEWING AND EMBELLISHING THE QUILT

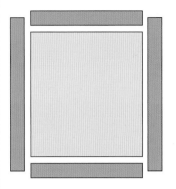

1. Sew the top and bottom borders to the pink center and press the seams toward the borders.

2. Add the side borders to the center and press the seams toward the borders.

3. Refer to the project photo on page 24 to see the layout for the images and frames. Layer the images and purple framing fabric on the nonstick appliqué pressing sheet and fuse the layers together.

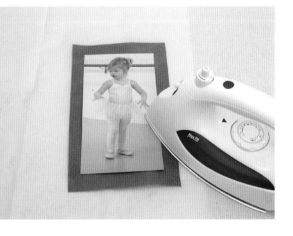

4. Arrange the framed images on the quilt center and fuse in place.

5. Layer the backing, batting, and quilt top.

6. Quilt as desired and bind the quilt with the remaining purple fabric. (For quilting and binding tips, see Quilting Basics, page 44.)

7. Attach ribbons and other embellishments.

the *printed word*
using text in your projects

W ith the use of your computer and word processing software, you can add personal messages to any project. It can be as simple as adding a large monogram printed on canvas, as in the monogram plaque. You can include a special note or sentimental song for your loved one. Or simply create fabulous backgrounds for your projects using a repeated word or phrase. Use the text box option in your word processing software to layer words on top of your image. Alternatively, some photo-editing software supports the use of layering to accomplish this effect.

L is for liam

—monogram plaque

Finished size: 12″ × 12″

I love to combine different fabrics, ribbons, and ephemera, as well as photos, other graphics, and fonts to create beautifully personalized home décor. I created this monogrammed wallhanging to match a lovely quilt that was given to Liam at birth. By incorporating a left-over fabric scrap from the quilt, I was able to create a piece that instantly coordinated with his room.

what you'll need

- 1 pretreated printable canvas peel-and-stick sheet, 8½″ × 11″
- 15″ × 15″ fabric scrap
- 2 Display Boards, 12″ × 12″ (Create & Treasure)
- 24″ black polka-dot ribbon, 1″ wide

- 42″ black ribbon, 1″ wide
- 6 black ribbons of varying widths (⅛″ to ½″-wide) in 6″ lengths
- 18″ black ribbon, ⅛″-wide for tying the letter
- Ghost letters (Heidi Swapp)
- Metal letter (or wood or papier-mâché)
- Japanese screw punch or hand drill
- Miracle Tape (Ranger Industries)
- Xyron machine with adhesive cartridge
- Glue Dots

how-to

1. Using the Xyron machine, place adhesive on the back of the 15″ × 15″ fabric scrap, creating a large fabric sticker. Because the fabric is so wide, you may have to fold the fabric in half, right sides facing each other, and feed it through the Xyron machine twice to place adhesive on the entire fabric back.

2. Lay the fabric with the adhesive side up on a cutting mat. Center a display board on the fabric, leaving 1½″ of fabric extending beyond the board on all sides. Press the board onto the fabric.

3. Miter the corners of fabric, making a diagonal cut at each corner approximately ¼″ from the display board corner, and then fold fabric over edges of display board.

4. Open your word processing program, select the desired font, type in a monogram, and size it to fit your printable fabric sheet. Plan the monogram to fill most of the space on the sheet, but leave room on the bottom right-hand corner for adding the metal letter.

5. Print the monogram on the printable canvas sheet.

6. Apply the monogram printed peel-and-stick canvas sheet, centering it on the front of the board.

7. To add the framing ribbons, refer to the project photo to see that 12″-long polka dot ribbons frame the top and bottom of the printed sheet and that 12″-long solid black ribbons frame the sides. Notice how the ribbons overlap at the corners in an alternating fashion: polka dot overlaps at the top left-hand corner, solid black at the top right-hand corner, polka dot at the bottom right-hand corner, and solid black at the bottom left-hand corner. Glue the ribbons in place with Glue Dots.

8. Using the Xyron machine, place adhesive on the back of the ghost letters and adhere to the fabric over the monogram.

9. Embellish the metal letter by knotting the 6″ lengths of ribbon around the letter. Refer to the project photo to see how I tied the ribbons.

10. Place the letter on the covered board and make 6 marks (3 per side) along the ribbon in the lower right corner of the board.

11. Remove the letter and punch holes in the display board with Japanese screw punch or hand drill.

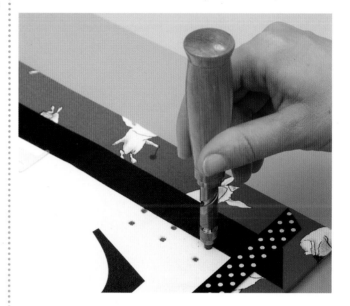

12. Cut the 18″ length of ⅛″-wide ribbon into 3 pieces. Through holes from the back, thread the ribbons to the front, wrap the ribbons around the letter, and then thread the ribbons to the back, tying the ribbons on the back to secure the letter to the display board.

13. Use an 18″-length of black ribbon to create the hanger at the top of the board. Put Miracle Tape along the top edge of the back of the board, securing the ends of the ribbon hanger. Put Miracle Tape along the remaining edges of the board and use the second display board as the backing to finish the project.

i hope you dance
—dollhouse shadow box

Finished size: 30″ × 30″

Ballerina photos by Scott Belding Photography

All parents have hopes and dreams for their children. This project is the perfect way to display fabulous photos of your little one, combined with a beautiful, personal message. I used the lyrics to a beautiful song, *I Hope You Dance* by Lee Ann Womack, to convey my wishes to my daughter. While I am thrilled that she dances, I really hope that she understands the underlying message of the lyrics as she gets older. I hope that she experiences life to the fullest and enjoys what the world has to offer. I hope she chooses to live her life out loud. This project is just for you, Ava, my love. I hope you dance.

what you'll need

- 5 photos
- 4 pretreated printable fabric sheets, 8½″ × 11″
- Unfinished dollhouse bookshelf, about 30″ × 30″ (I found this one at Michaels.)
- 3 sheets printed scrapbook papers, 12″ × 12″
- 5 yards crushed velvet ribbon, ¼″-wide
- Papier-mâché body form, 12″-tall (Creative Imaginations)

- Ballet slippers
- Wand
- *I Hope You Dance* book and CD (Book is available from Stampington & Company. I added Ava's photos to the cover.)
- 6 silk roses (Dulken & Derrick Inc.)
- Black chalkboard paint
- Tattered Rose and Antique Linen Distress Inks (Ranger Industries)
- Off-white acrylic paint
- Tea dye
- Foam brush
- Alphabet stamps
- Wish card, 2″ × 3½″ (7 Gypsies)
- Doll-sized tutu
- BeJeweler Pro (Creative Crystals)
- Swarovski crystals (Creative Crystals)
- Small jar filled with pearl buttons
- Metal "Wonder" charm, 2″ × 2″
- Miracle Tape (Ranger Industries)
- Xyron machine with adhesive cartridge
- Glue gun
- Tacky glue
- Masking tape
- Craft knife

how-to

THE DOLLHOUSE, PHOTOS, AND BOOK

1. Apply 2–3 coats of black chalkboard paint to the dollhouse bookshelf, inside and outside. Allow paint to dry between coats, according to the manufacturer's instructions.

2. Look at the project photo (page 29) to see how the outside of the house is embellished with words. Using a foam brush to apply off-white acrylic paint to stamps, stamp words. Allow the paint to dry completely. I used words and phrases from the lyrics of "I Hope You Dance" by Lee Ann Womack.

3. Cover the front edges of all the shelves, roofline, and sides of the dollhouse with the crushed velvet ribbon, using tacky glue. This creates frames for all the vignettes.

4. Following the manufacturer's instructions, print photos on fabric sheets to the following sizes: 1 at 5″ × 7″ (photo of dancer, printed in portrait layout); 1 at 5″ × 7″ (photo of dancer and teacher, printed in landscape layout); and 2 at 4″ × 6″ (close-ups of dancer, to be cropped to fit book covers).

5. Use photo-editing software to add poetry text of your choice to the photo portrait, to be printed at 8″ × 10″. Print this on the last fabric sheet.

6. To personalize the book, apply the 4″ × 6″ photos to the front and back covers, trimming the photos to fit your book. I taped the photos to the front and back book cover with pieces of torn masking tape.

7. Cut 2 sheets of 12″ × 12″ scrapbook paper into quarters, creating 8 squares, each 6″ × 6″. These will be used to embellish the vignettes.

LOWER LEFT VIGNETTE

1. Distress the wand and the papier-mâché body form with both distress inks, rubbing the inks directly onto the objects until the desired effect is achieved.

2. Once the inks have dried thoroughly, apply Swarovski crystals to the wand, using the BeJewler Pro tool, according to the manufacturer's instructions.

3. Tea-dye the tutu by soaking it in dye overnight. Place the dry tea-dyed tutu on the papier-mâché body form.

4. Adhere the remaining 12″ × 12″ scrapbook paper to the background of the vignette, using Miracle Tape. Refer to the project photo for placement.

5. Place the 8″ × 10″ photo with text on the background sheet, using Xyron adhesive.

6. Adhere the wand at the left of the photo, using the hot glue gun.

7. Set the body form in the vignette to the right of the photo.

TOP RIGHT VIGNETTE

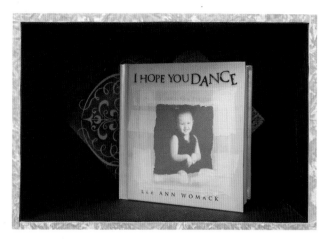

1. Using Miracle Tape, adhere 2 pieces of 6″ × 6″ scrapbook paper to the back of the vignette. Refer to the project photo for placement. Trim the excess paper edges using a craft knife.

2. Place the *I Hope You Dance* book in the vignette.

BOTTOM RIGHT VIGNETTE

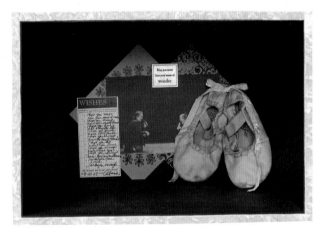

1. Adhere 2 sheets of 6″ × 6″ scrapbook paper, using Miracle Tape, to the back of the vignette. Refer to the project photo for placement. Trim the excess paper edges using a craft knife.

2. Apply adhesive with a Xyron machine to the 5″ × 7″ landscape-oriented photo. Position this on the scrapbook paper.

3. Adhere metal "Wonder" charm at the top of the photo, using Miracle Tape.

4. Add personal wishes to the *Wishes* card and place it to the left of the photo, using Miracle Tape.

5. Place the ballet slippers in the right corner of the vignette.

> ***tip** Because the theme of my project is dance, I pinned my daughter's first pair of ballet slippers together and pinned a bow at the top of the slippers. Other ideas include bronzed ballet slippers, bronzed or plain baby shoes, cowboy boots, and hats.

TOP VIGNETTE

1. Adhere 4 sheets of 6″ × 6″ scrapbook paper, using Miracle Tape, to the back of the vignette. Refer to the project photo for placement. Trim the excess paper edges using a craft knife.

2. Trim the top edges of the 5″ × 7″ portrait-oriented photo to fit under the roof at the back. Apply adhesive to the photo using the Xyron machine and place the photo in the vignette.

3. Place silk flowers in the left corner and a small jar of buttons in the right corner.

> ***tip** You can add a pocket to the back of the dollhouse to hold the program from your child's first performance.

AVA you're a doll!
—display board with paper dolls

By Phyllis Nelson
Finished size: 12″ × 12″

What little girl doesn't love to make believe? This is the perfect gift for the imaginative little one in your life. Phyllis made this fabulous card for her granddaughter. It features a take-along "home," with paper doll and wardrobe. A personal message and the child's name were printed on pre-treated printable fabric using a word processing program, making the gift even more special. What a great gift idea that can be taken along to keep little ones occupied during road trips, at restaurants, or anywhere else you can dream up!

what you'll need

- 3 pretreated printable peel-and-stick fabric sheets, 8½″ × 11″
- Display Board, 12″ × 12″ (Create & Treasure)
- 1 sheet light blue cardstock, 12″ × 12″
- 1 sheet white cardstock, 12″ × 12″
- 1 sheet white cardstock, 8½″ × 11″
- 1 sheet silver cardstock, 12″ × 12″
- 1 sheet vellum, 8½″ × 11″
- 1 sheet dark blue cardstock, 8½″ × 11″
- 2 yards dotted ribbon, ¼″ wide
- Royal blue acrylic paint
- Decorative corner and hinge die cuts (Sizzix)
- 2″ oval scallop nameplate punch (or design it freehand)
- 2½″ oval nameplate punch (or design them freehand)
- Corner-rounder punch
- Keyhole sticker (This one is by Frances Meyer or create your own.)
- 5 white mini brads
- 6″ silver cord, ⅛″ diameter
- Rub-on, sticker, or die-cut alphabet lettering
- Paper doll and wardrobe
- Double-sided tape
- Xyron machine with adhesive cartridge
- Glue Dots

how-to

BACK COVER   **FRONT COVER**

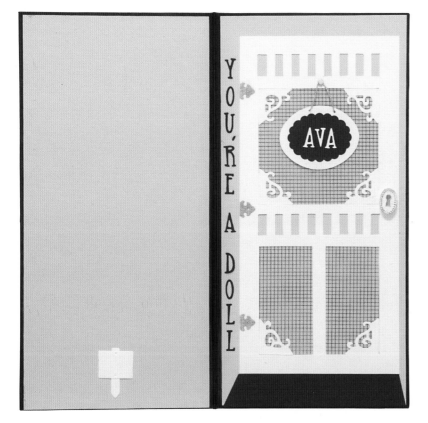

1. Use the royal blue acrylic paint to paint all of the display board—front, back, and edges. Allow paint to dry completely according to the manufacturer's instructions.

2. Cut 2 pieces of light blue cardstock to 5¾″ × 11¾″.

3. Cut a door 5″ × 10¼″ from the 8½″ × 11″ white cardstock and draw the 3¾″ × 3½″ window 1½″ down from the top. Then cut out the side panels ½″ from the bottom, each 1⅝″ × 3¼″. The small blue ¼″ × ⅝″ details can be cut out of the door; or to make it easier, cut each detail from light blue cardstock and glue to the door.

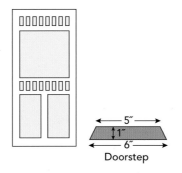

Doorstep

4. Cut the doorstep from dark blue cardstock. The door step is 1″ high, 5″ across the top, and 6″ at the bottom. See the project photo.

5. Using the die cuts, cut 6 decorative corners from white cardstock scraps and 3 hinges from the silver cardstock.

6. Print a grid on the vellum sheet to create the "screen." (Phyllis created her grid with an Excel spreadsheet, but you could use some real screen from the hardware store.)

7. Punch pieces for the nameplate from white (2½″ oval) and dark blue (2″ scallop oval) cardstock. Cut letters for your child's name from the white cardstock. Glue the nameplate layers together and add the name lettering, using Xyron adhesive. Attach the silver cord to the nameplate as shown in the photo and hang the nameplate on a white mini brad inserted into the door.

8. Arrange all the cut-outs on the display board front, referring to the project photo. When you are pleased with the layout, adhere all the paper pieces using Xyron adhesive, layering the papers where necessary.

9. Adhere the keyhole sticker, using Glue Dots.

10. Use rub-on or sticker alphabet letters for "YOU'RE A DOLL"—or die-cut the lettering from the blue cardstock—for the left side of the door.

11. You can see a "white sign on a post" on the lower left side of the outside photo. You can fashion your own "sign" to use for your signature as the creator of this project.

INSIDE

8. Punch the white "Happy Birthday" sign, with an oval scallop punch. Punch a dark blue oval.

> ✱ **tip** To ensure that the words are centered on your sign, turn your punch over so that your message is visible through the hole in the punch, and center before punching.

9. Cut a light blue rectangle 2¼" × 3¼" for the first background of the "Happy Birthday" sign. Use a corner rounder to trim corners.

10. Cut a dark blue rectangle 2½" × 3½" for the second background of the "Happy Birthday" sign.

11. Adhere all the layers of the "Happy Birthday" sign, using Xyron adhesive. Put the white mini brads through the corners as shown in the photo. Then adhere the sign to the display board, positioning as shown.

12. Insert the paper doll and wardrobe into pockets for your special little one to enjoy.

1. Print "you're a doll" in a repeating pattern with blue ink on 2 sheets of pretreated printable fabric sheets, following the manufacturer's instructions.

2. Cut 2 pieces 5¾" × 11¾" from the printed fabric. Remove the backing and adhere it to the display board, referring to the project photo for placement.

3. Print the child's name with blue ink in a repeating pattern, using a variety of fonts on the remaining pretreated printable fabric sheet.

4. Cut 2 pieces of white cardstock 5" × 5¾". Trim a 5¾" side at an angle to create the pockets. Remove the backing from the fabric and apply the fabric to the cardstock. Trim the fabric to fit the cardstock. Attach the fabric-covered cardstock to the lower corners with double-sided tape on the bottom and sides, as shown in the photo. Leave the top edges unattached to form pockets.

5. Frame pockets with ribbon, attaching with double-sided tape.

6. Cut 2 decorative corners from dark blue cardstock for the upper corners.

7. Print "Happy Birthday" in blue ink on white cardstock.

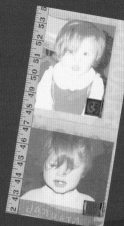

photo-editing
techniques &
printing on fabric

If you have digital images, an all-in-one printer, and some basic photo-editing software, there are a number of fabulous effects you can apply to your images. To adjust the colors of your image, you can alter the hue and saturation, manipulate the brightness and contrast, and change from color images to black and white or sepia. You can also add a number of interesting effects, such as *posterize, ripple, brick texture, oil painting, neon edges*, and many more. Before starting your project, familiarize yourself with the capabilities of your photo-editing software, as they are all slightly different in their operations. From the examples in this chapter, you can see some of the incredible effects that many photo-editing software programs offer.

photo-editing effects

Here are some of the fabulous effects that many photo-editing software programs have to offer.

Original Image

Colored Pencil

Emboss

Bas Relief

Cutout

Extrude

Chalk Charcoal

Diffuse Glow

Fresco

Glowing Edges

Photocopy

Solarize

Halftone

Pinch—Negative

Twirl

Neon Glow

Pinch—Positive

> **✱tip** *Once you have selected images for your projects, it is a good idea to save a copy of them to a "work in progress" folder, so that you can maintain the integrity of the original image.*

they grow so fast
—growth chart

Finished size: 6˝ × 60˝

Children grow so fast. A fun and decorative way to capture their growth is with this personalized growth chart. While my photos display Ava's growth in just ten short months (I chose to use photos from between 6 months and 15 months old), the chart can be used to track their height until they reach 60˝.

what you'll need

- 10 photos
- 4–5 pretreated printable fabric peel-and-stick sheets, 8½˝ × 11˝
- 2 Accordion Blank Board books, 6˝ × 6˝ (Create & Treasure)
- 8 pieces of scrapbook paper, 6˝ × 6˝
- 2 pieces of scrapbook paper, 6˝ × 6½˝
- 3 yards ⅛˝-wide ribbon
- Metal charms (Making Memories)
- 60˝ measuring tape
- Japanese screw punch or hand drill
- Xyron machine with adhesive cartridge
- Miracle Tape
- Glue Dots

how-to

1. Spread an Accordion Board Book flat on your work surface and you will see that there are 5 sections per Accordion Board Book—4 pages measuring 6″ x 6″ and 1 page measuring 6″ x 6 ½″. The 6″ x 6 ½″ page will be the top page of the lower half of the growth chart. This will be Book 1.

2. Using the Xyron machine, put adhesive on the back of a 6″ x 6″ piece of scrapbook paper, creating a large sticker. Align the edges of paper and the Accordion Board Book page as you apply the sticker. Repeat for the next 3 sections of Book 1.

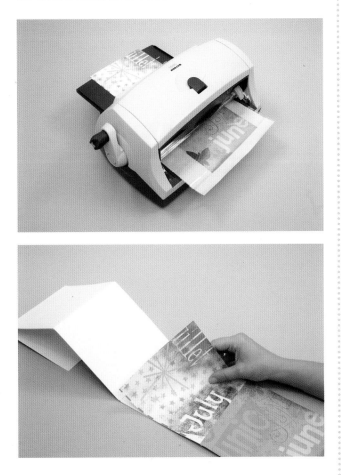

3. Using the Xyron machine, make a sticker with a 6″ x 6½″ piece of scrapbook paper for the top page of Book 1. Align the edges of paper and the Accordion Board Book page as you apply the sticker.

4. Repeat Steps 1–3 for Accordion Board Book 2. This second book creates the upper half of the growth chart.

5. Print desired photos on printable fabric sheets, following the manufacturer's instructions. The Accordion Board Book pages are 6″ x 6″, so plan accordingly. I printed 10 different photos of varying sizes to fit on the pages.

6. Trim photos to fit each page of the growth chart. Arrange the photos on the growth chart and then peel-and-stick them to the pages.

7. Adhere metal charms using Glue Dots.

8. Punch holes using a Japanese screw punch or hand drill along the top page of Book 1 and the bottom page of Book 2.

9. Lace ribbons through the holes to tie Book 1 and Book 2 together.

10. Use Miracle Tape to adhere measuring tape to the left side of the growth chart.

> ✳**tip** *If you find that the peel-and-stick printable fabric is too transparent once the backing paper has been removed, it can be mounted to white cardstock. Then the cardstock backing can be secured to the chart with Xyron adhesive. This prevents the background paper or fabric from showing through the printable fabric sheet. Note that this can only be done with projects that do not require washing.*

pappa joe
—puzzle block box

By Vanessa O'Neal
Finished size: 5″ × 5″

This is the perfect gift for anyone with whom you'd like to share your cherished memories. This puzzle block box features six different photos of your choice. It's great for your children, as they can solve puzzles while looking at pictures of loved ones. It's also great for parents, grandparents, teachers, or just decorating your home, as it is a unique way to display photos. My puzzle block box features photos of Ava and Liam with their grandpa, Pappa Joe, during a fun outing. I adjusted the color balance of each photo to help the little ones learn different colors while solving the puzzles.

what you'll need

- 6 photos with color balance adjusted to varying tints
- 2 pretreated printable fabric peel-and-stick sheets, 8½″ × 11″
- Unfinished wood box with hinged lid, 5″ × 5″
- 4 unfinished wood blocks, 2″ × 2″
- 1 piece of polka-dot scrapbook paper, 4¼″ × 4¼″
- 1 piece of patterned scrapbook paper, 4¼″ × 4¼″
- Alphabet stickers (SEI)
- Frame sticker, 3″ × 3″ (SEI)
- *My Special Memories* sticker, 1½″ × 1½″ (SEI)
- 1 coaster with a G, 3″ × 3″ (SEI)
- Plum EZ Walnut Ink TintZ (Fiber Scraps)
- Acrylic paint
- Rub-on words and phrases
- Buttons
- Xyron machine with adhesive cartridge
- Glue Dots
- Craft knife
- Sponge

how-to

OUTSIDE

1. Paint the entire box inside and outside, using acrylic paint. Allow paint to dry completely, according to the manufacturer's instructions.

2. Apply rub-on words and phrases to sides of the box as desired, according to the manufacturer's instructions.

3. Distress the outside of the box by dispensing a small amount of walnut ink into a plastic palette and applying with a dry sponge.

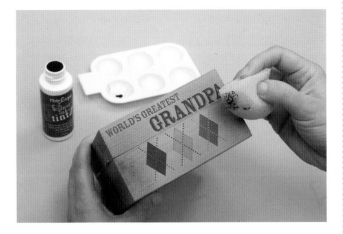

4. Use the Xyron machine to apply adhesive to the polka-dot paper to make a large sticker. Apply the sticker to the top of the box lid.

5. Place the frame sticker and *My Special Memories* sticker in the center of the polka-dot sheet as shown in the project photo.

6. Adhere buttons to the bottom right of the lid frame, using glue dots.

INSIDE

1. Using the Xyron machine, apply adhesive to the patterned paper to make a large sticker. Apply the sticker to the inside of the lid.

2. Apply rub-on words and letters to the patterned paper. Adhere the coaster with Glue Dots and add the alphabet stickers, as shown.

3. Adhere buttons on the coaster, using Glue Dots.

4. Print 4 photos, approximately 4″ × 4″, per sheet on pretreated printable peel-and-stick fabric sheets, following the manufacturer's instructions.

5. Trim each photo to 4″ × 4″.

6. Place 4 unfinished blocks together (2 across, 2 down) on a firm surface and apply the peel-and-stick photo to the 4-block group. Cut the blocks apart using a craft knife.

7. Turn all blocks to expose an unfinished side and repeat Step 6. Repeat for the remaining photos/block sides.

8. Distress the edges of the blocks using walnut ink on a dry sponge.

9. Place the completed blocks in the wooden container.

one year, many moments
—scrapbook clock

Finished size: 12˝ diameter

Time flies. With my son Liam's birthday around the corner, I had to take a moment and recall the many moments of his first year of life. I included a favorite photo converted to black and white then printed on fabric, background ribbon with a happy birthday message, and tags highlighting the momentous dates of his first bath, word, haircut, tooth, and first step. For me, this clock holds many memories and serves as a reminder that I should cherish these moments, as time truly does fly.

what you'll need

- 1 digital photo image
- Photo-editing software
- 1 pretreated printable fabric sheet, 8½˝ × 11˝
- 12˝-diameter clock and acetate overlay (Heidi Swapp)
- 1 sheet black cardstock, 12˝ × 12˝
- 1 sheet black cardstock, 8½˝ × 11˝
- 20 ribbons in 12˝ lengths in varying widths (¼˝ to ¾˝ wide)

- 5 metal charms, ¼˝ high
- White Market Tag (Pebbles Inc.) or use your own plastic bread tag
- Mini Tags die and die cutter (Sizzix)
- Mini brads
- White gel pen
- Adhesives (I prefer Xyron for adhering ribbons, Herma Dotto for paper, and Glue Dots for adhering metal charms.)

how-to

1. Trace acetate overlay onto 12˝ square of black cardstock and trim.

✱tip Save the scraps of black cardstock for cutting mini tags later in this project.

2. On your computer, open the photo and crop to 6″ × 6″.

3. Print your photo onto the fabric sheet, according to the manufacturer's instructions.

> ✳ *tip* *When positioning the photo, be sure the clock movements won't cover the main image.*

4. Trim the photo and sew decorative stitching around it, if desired.

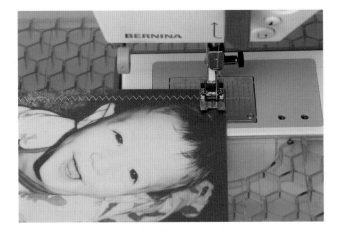

5. From the remaining cardstock, cut a piece to match the photo size.

6. As shown, adhere ribbons to the cardstock using your favorite adhesive. (I used a Xyron machine on the cardstock and finger-pressed the ribbons to the cardstock.) Trim the ribbons as desired.

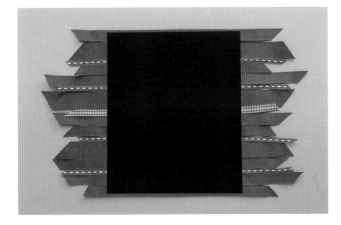

7. Using the Xyron machine, glue the photo to the ribbon background. Write "Smile" on the market tag and place it at the bottom right corner of photo. Use Glue Dots to secure the tag.

8. Lay the acetate overlay down. Attach black die-cut mini tags to metal charms, using the small brads. Write on the black tags with a white gel pen. Place metal charms with tags on the acetate overlay and glue pieces down using Glue Dots.

9. Assemble the clock, according to the manufacturer's instructions.

> ✳ *tip* *If you find that your clock hands get stuck on dimensional items that are placed on top of your overlay, insert an additional washer to the clock movements so that your clock hands will clear the 3D items.*

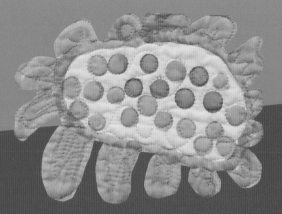

quilting basics

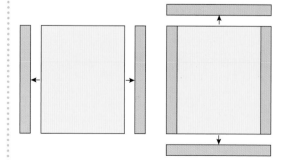

Fabric requirements in this book are based on a 42″ width. It is always a good idea to prewash your fabrics before beginning a project. Many fabrics shrink when washed, and widths vary by manufacturer. In the cutting instructions, strips are generally cut on the crosswise grain.

seam allowances

A ¼″ seam allowance is used for most projects. It's a good idea to do a test seam before you begin sewing to check that your ¼″ is accurate.

pressing

In general, press seams toward the darker fabric. Press lightly in an up-and-down motion. Avoid using a very hot iron or over ironing, which can distort shapes and blocks.

straight-cut borders

In most cases, the side borders are sewn to the quilt center first. Once you have finished the quilt center, measure vertically through the center. This will be the length to cut the side borders. Place pins at the centers of all four sides of the quilt top, as well as in the center of each side border strip. Pin the side borders to the quilt top first, matching the center pins. Using a ¼″ seam allowance, sew the borders to the quilt top and press.

Measure horizontally through the center of the quilt top, including the side borders. This will be the length to cut the top and bottom borders. Repeat pinning, sewing, and pressing.

backing

Plan on making the backing a minimum of 4″ larger than the quilt top. Prewash and iron the fabric and trim the selvages (finished edges) before you piece the backing. To economize, you can piece the back from any scraps or leftover blocks in your collection.

batting

The type of batting to use is a personal decision; consult your local quilt shop. Cut batting approximately 4″ larger than your quilt top.

layering

1. Spread the backing wrong side up and tape the edges down with masking tape. (If you are working on carpet, you can use T-pins to secure the backing to the carpet.)

2. Center the batting on top, smoothing out any folds.

3. Place the quilt top right side up on top of the batting and backing, making sure it's centered.

basting

If you plan to machine quilt, pin baste the quilt layers together with safety pins a minimum of 3″–4″ apart. Begin basting in the center and move toward the edges—first in vertical, then horizontal rows.

If you plan to hand quilt, baste the layers together with thread using a long needle and light-colored thread. Knot one end of the thread. Using stitches approximately the length of the needle, begin in the center and move out toward the edges.

quilting

Quilting, whether by hand or machine, enhances the pieced or appliquéd design of the quilt. You may choose to echo the pieced or appliquéd motifs, use patterns from quilting design books and stencils, or do your own free-motion quilting.

binding

DOUBLE-FOLD STRAIGHT-GRAIN BINDING (FRENCH FOLD)

1. Trim excess batting and backing from the quilt. If you want a ¼″ finished binding, cut the strips 2″ wide and piece together with a diagonal seam to make a continuous binding strip.

2. Press the seams open, then press the entire strip in half lengthwise with wrong sides together. Trim one end of the binding strip at a 45° angle and press under the trimmed end ¼″. This is your starting end.

3. With raw edges even, pin the binding to the edge of the quilt a few inches away from a corner. Leave the first 3″ of the binding unattached. Start sewing, using a ¼″ seam allowance. Stop ¼″ away from the first corner and backstitch one stitch. Lift the presser foot and remove the quilt from under the needle. Rotate the quilt 90°.

Stitch to ¼″ from corner.

4. Fold the binding at a right angle so it extends straight above the quilt and the fold forms a 45° angle in the corner.

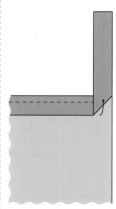

First fold for miter

5. Bring the binding strip down even with the edge of the quilt. Begin sewing at the folded edge. Continue around the quilt and repeat in the same manner at each corner.

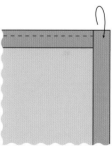

Second fold alignment

6. When you reach the binding starting point, tuck the end into the starting end and trim away the excess. Continue sewing the binding to the quilt.

7. Fold the binding over the raw edges to the quilt back and hand stitch, mitering the corners.

sources

Thank you to the following vendors for providing the products that made the projects possible:

MICHAEL MILLER FABRICS
212.704.0774
www.michaelmillerfabrics.com

CREATIVE CRYSTAL COMPANY
941.365.3006
www.creative-crystal.com

EK SUCCESS
800.524.1349
www.eksuccess.com

FIBER SCRAPS
215.230.4905
www.fiberscraps.com

HAMBLY SCREEN PRINTS
408.496.1100
www.hamblyscreenprints.com

KAREN FOSTER DESIGN
801.451.9779
www.karenfosterdesign.com

KRYLON PRODUCTS GROUP
800.457.9566
www.krylon.com

SEI
435.752.4142
www.shopsei.com

RANGER INDUSTRIES INC.
732.389.3535
www.rangerink.com

ADDITIONAL SOURCES
7 GYPSIES
877.749.7797
www.sevengypsies.com

AMERICAN CRAFTS
801.226.0747
www.americancrafts.com

BUBBLE JET SET 2000
314.521.7544
www.cjenkinscompany.com

CREATIVE IMAGINATIONS
www.creativeimaginations.us

DULKEN & DERRICK SILK FLOWERS
212.929.3614
www.flowersinthecity.com

HEIDI SWAPP BY ADVANTUS CORP.
904.482.0092
www.heidiswapp.com

JENNIFER CHANEY PHOTOGRAPHY
www.jchaney.com

MAKING MEMORIES
801.294.0430
www.makingmemories.com

MAY ARTS
203.637.8366
www.mayarts.com

MAYA ROAD
877.427.7764
www.mayaroad.com

PEBBLES INC.
801.235.1520
www.pebblesinc.com

PROVO CRAFT
800.937.7686
www.provocraft.com

QUICKUTZ
801.765.1144
www.quickutz.com

RUSTOLEUM
800.323.3584
www.rustoleum.com

SCOTT BELDING PHOTOGRAPHY
925.938.3300
www.scottbeldingphotography.com

SIZZIX
877.355.4766
www.sizzix.com

STAMPER'S ANONYMOUS
800.945.3980
www.stampersanonymous.com

STAMPINGTON & COMPANY
877.STAMPER (877.782.6737)
www.stampington.com

TREND ENTERPRISES INC.
800.860.6762
www.trendenterprises.com

XYRON, INC.
800.793.3523
www.xyron.com

BIBLIOGRAPHY

Photo Fun: Print Your Own Fabric for Quilts & Crafts. The Hewlett-Packard Company, edited by Cyndy Lyle Rymer. C&T Publishing, Lafayette, CA, 2004.

More Photo Fun: Exciting New Ideas for Printing on Fabric for Quilts & Crafts. Cyndy Lyle Rymer and Lynn Koolish. C&T Publishing, Lafayette, CA, 2005.

Fast Fun & Easy® Scrapbook Quilts: Create a Keepsake for Every Memory. Sue Astroth. C&T Publishing, Lafayette, CA, 2004.

Spectacular Cards: Fabric, Paper & Game Board Greetings. Sue Astroth. C&T Publishing, Lafayette, CA, 2005.

Super-Simple Creative Costumes. Sue Astroth. C&T Publishing, Lafayette, CA, 2006.

about the author

Photo by Jennifer Chaney

Krista Camacho Halligan was born in Tamuning, Guam. She has lived in many different places around the world, but finally settled in Northern California where she now lives with her husband, Mitchell, and her favorite small people, Allison, Ava, and Liam.

Privileged to work and teach classes at a local stamp, art, and scrapbook store, Krista met many fabulous artists and was exposed to a variety of mediums. Her work has been featured in many publications, including *Spectacular Cards*, *Make Spectacular Books*, and *Super-Simple Creative Costumes* from C&T Publishing, alongside *Scrapbooks & Beyond* and *Hidden Treasures*.

Upon the arrival of some small people, Krista's artistic career took a backseat to motherhood. She is now a very content (and tremendously busy) stay-at-home mom who squeezes art in between dance, music, gymnastics, preschool, and potty training (the small people, that is).

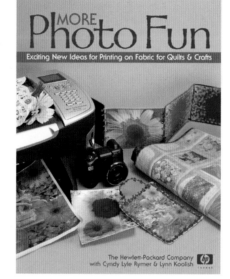

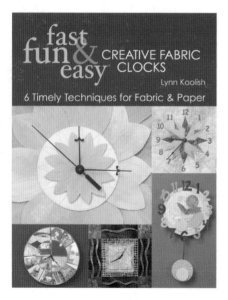

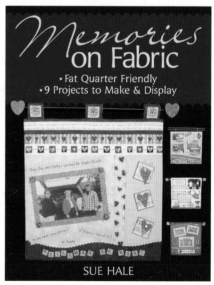